THE
SIMPLE LIFE

Discipline For Modern Day Clergy

M.C. TOLBERT

iUniverse, Inc.
Bloomington

The Simple Life
Discipline For Modern Day Clergy

Copyright © 2011 M.C. Tolbert

iUniverse books may be ordered through booksellers or by contacting:

iUniverse
1663 Liberty Drive
Bloomington, IN 47403
www.iuniverse.com
1-800-Authors (1-800-288-4677)

ISBN: 978-1-4620-4358-3 (sc)
ISBN: 978-1-4620-4359-0 (e)

Printed in the United States of America

iUniverse rev. date: 8/3/2011

CONTENTS

Bible Reference Key

(HCSB)	Holman Christian Standard Bible
(NIV)	New International Version
(NRSV)	New Revised Standard Version
(KJV)	King James Version

INTRODUCTION

All of us need someone who can mentor us and inspire us to lean forward in our Christian faith. Even clergy need someone to give them encouragement from time to time. I suppose I am seeking to be a preachers' preacher in this writing. My wish is to encourage clergy so we can "keep on keeping on" in our work of building the Kingdom of God. Many clergy have shipwrecked on the island of failure and despair in the journey of ministry. Neither seminary nor early experience in the church gives us all the insight we need about doing ministry and how to be most effective in our particular area. Having a coach who seeks to keep us accountable can be very beneficial. I have had several mentors during my years of ministry, and they have been most helpful to me.

Clergy talk a lot about discipline but often lack it in some important areas of their lives. I am not making judgment calls. I am only giving what I consider words of encouragement, as I reflect on my learning experiences during the years of my public ministry. I realize that clergy will have different responses to specific situations in ministry, but there are some common disciplines we need to pursue. Having effective ministry is most important to clergy, who see themselves as, "ambassadors for Christ" (2 Corinthians 5:20,HCSB).

All too often, clergy allow "the little foxes that spoil the vine" (Song of Solomon 2:15, KJV) to roam free in their everyday journeys of ministry. Clergy want to know why they are not more productive in God's work. Taking a close look at some of the pitfalls in ministry can help us cut off some of our defeats. We can also cut down clergy exhaustion and burnout. My desire is to benefit clergy by making some suggestions on how we can manage our ministries more closely.

In this writing, I cover the following topics: (1) defining "simple",

(2) the voice of God, (3) having joy in our work, (4) clergy and wealth, (5) meeting the world, (6) having a heart for ministry, and (7) being a servant.

My prayer is that this writing will be enjoyable reading for you. May it provide strength and inspiration to you on your journey of ministry.

ACKNOWLEDGMENTS

Thanks to my wife, Anna, who lovingly supported me in this writing, showed patience as I referenced and wrote for hours, and prodded me when I got slow. Thanks to so many professors who, through my years of education in religion and theology, inspired me to be all I could be. Thanks to my dear friend, Larry Blann, who proofread my manuscript and encouraged me to publish it.

CHAPTER

1

Defining "Simple"

W hen we hear the word "simple" as it pertains to our lifestyles, most of us think about the poor, those who live in some underprivileged area of the world, or at least about those who are not fortunate enough to have some of the needed accessories to make life comfortable. There are also those persons who have chosen to live a *modest* lifestyle in order to keep them from being covetous or what some call "too worldly." These are some of the terms we might hear in the Christian societies or church communities around us. As Christians, we have to make choices about our lifestyles and whether they are acceptable to God or need some changes. Clergy are no exception to this type of examination. In fact, we ought to be the leaders in seeking to please God in our lifestyles.

Throughout my years of public ministry, I have seen many clergy who were committed to living modestly and many others who lived rather lavishly. Some clergy didn't have a choice about their modest lifestyles, because they had modest income. Others fared better and lived a little more on the upper-class level. At this point, I am not eager to make any speeches about setting limits on clergy income, but I do desire to speak to the need of having a *simple life* ministry. I believe that living the simple life can cover the whole gamut of clergy life.

First of all, I want to give some dictionary definitions of "simple" and then to look at each one separately, applying the concepts to Christian ministry. Next, I will speak of a personal definition of "living simply." Four definitions are: (1) having or consisting of only one part, feature, substance; (2) not complicated or involved; (3) pure, unadulterated; (4) of low rank or position (Webster's New World Dictionary).

Having or consisting of only one part, feature, substance. Matthew 6:24 (NRSV) says, "No one can serve two masters, Either he will hate the one and love the other, or he will be devoted to the one and despise the other. You cannot serve both God and Money." The word "money," or "mammon," is used to identify negative accumulations. Jesus did not want his disciples to be concerned with gathering treasures in this life but to store up treasures in heaven. We can use these words of Jesus to his disciples to give us guidance in our ministries and to help us know where our priorities should be.

I believe this definition of simple can help us to realize Christ should not be divided, but we should keep him as one. In other words, we could make a strong argument for the Trinity here. Jesus and God the Father are one (cf. John 17), and we should be one with them. We can be one with them in the Spirit. We can have some of the same features—at least the spiritual features—Jesus had. Galatians 5:22 lists the fruits of the Spirit that we should possess. Jesus possessed these fruits of the Spirit. We can have the same substance with the Father, Son, and Spirit. No, not the *deified* substance they possess, but we can have the *holy* substance. We can be committed to living holy lives. As clergy, our goal should be to bring glory and honor to God with our lives. In this sense, we can consider ourselves one part or one with God. When we realize that only in the Holy Spirit are we one with God, we will seek to bring honor to him with our lives. If we have many goals to reach at one time (including those of our own making), we might not be able to focus on the main one. Our main goal should be to please God with our ministry. Of course, we have different areas of ministry in play at one time, and we must prioritize in order to do justice to any one of them. In our ministries, we have daily goals to reach, and we must stay focused on Christ so we can reach them.

Not complicated or involved. Someone has said that we need to, "keep it simple." This has been expressed in various contexts to show that persons understand the subject matter better when someone expresses it simply: in lay terms. Clergy are much better off when they preach, teach, and counsel using simple language. Of course, there are those times when we can insert some of our seminary language into the event just to keep the academicians happy. We have the right to be theology students, learning the deep things of Christian understanding and being able to describe Christian experiences in seminary or theological language. But we don't need to make the gospel message a complicated thing. From my understanding of the scriptures, Jesus doesn't want the gospel to become complicated: he wants it to stay simple. When he seemed to be above the disciples' heads at times, he would give parables (illustrations) to help them to get the picture clearly.

Sometimes, clergy complicate their lives through extreme involvement in community projects or organizations outside the church. We find that we have no time for our family or friends. They have to make appointments to see us. I believe this is complicating our lifestyle to the point of frustration for ourselves and others. It is almost impossible not to become involved with church denominational committees and outside organizations. Those committees and organizations stay alive by getting officers and leaders like us. However, we need to be so assertive as to say when enough is enough. It is honorable for us to serve outside our local church or ministry, but we must make sure that our called ministry comes first. Living the simple life as clergy means that we never get involved with these organizations just to make a greater name for ourselves. The more education and training we get, the more appealing we seem to be to civic groups. While we need to take the opportunities to help our communities, we need to know our limits and when it is appropriate to say no. We need to know when we should say no and not feel guilty about it.

Pure, unadulterated. Romans 3:23 (NIV) tells us, "for all have sinned and fall short of the glory of God". In this view, we know that we are not pure, at least in ourselves. Being pure means that we are not mixed with anything else. We are mixed with the taint of sin because of the original sin (The Fall) and, therefore, are impure. We stand in need of a deliverer from this sinful state. Jesus was, and still is, that deliverer. First John 1:9 (NRSV) says, "If we confess our sins, he is faithful and just and will forgive our sins and purify us from all unrighteousness". In our confession of sins, we are forgiven and made pure. James 1:27

(KJV) reads, "Pure religion and undefiled before God and the Father is this: to visit the fatherless and widows in their affliction, and to keep himself unspotted from the world." To keep oneself unspotted from the world is to be unadulterated. It is to obey God and keep his laws. It is to be committed to him completely. It is total fidelity. Clergy need to keep close tabs on their lives so they can be committed to their calling. I believe that part of the simple life for clergy is visiting the fatherless and widows in their affliction. Much of this duty has been delegated to social organizations, but clergy would do well to remember these persons and seek to be of help to them.

Of low rank or position. We sometimes think of low-ranking officers and leaders as the least important, but when we look at the overall structure and the duties involved, we realize all levels of leadership are important, not just those high positions. We need leaders, those who can inspire and direct, but we also need laborers, those who have hands-on experience, if we are going to have an organized business. Clergy are in *business* for God. It is a big business. Most of us are taught, trained, and educated to reach for the high positions. We find with the high positions comes a large responsibility. Sometimes, it is so large that we do not feel like we can accomplish it. In Romans 12:3, (NRSV) Paul says, "I say to every one of you: Do not think of yourself more highly than you ought, but rather think of yourself with sober judgment" . Even the clergy need to be humbled by their positions, knowing they came to them through the grace of God. Philippians 2:3 (NRSV) tells us, "Do nothing out of selfish ambition or vain conceit, but in humility consider others better than yourselves". To live simple means to be humbled about any position we have. We should give our very best to whatever task we are called to do. As clergy, we will not always be respected for our positions, but we can respect God in all we do and say. Let us serve others well. I will say more about being a servant in chapter 7.

In the process of gathering information for my book, I talked with several people to get their views about the simple life. One of these persons, Betty Shirley, a pastor, wrote me a definition of the simple life:

> Living simply has more to do with the condition of our hearts
> than it does with our physical situation. The heart committed
> to "walking with" the Lord is not driven by personal wants

but rather is waiting for instructions and empowerment for that which we have been and are being called to do ... We each have the option of living our lives our own way in a very competitive society or choosing to allow God to lead us in how he wants us to live.

"How liberating it is to acknowledge that He is in control and knows what is best" (Proverbs 3:5–6).

I really like Betty's definition. It is a well-worded statement about the simple life. The condition of our heart is most important. Matthew 5:8 (NIV) says, "Blessed are the pure in heart, for they will see God." Having purity of heart definitely places us high on God's pleasure list. A pure heart will lead us onto right paths so that we will seek instructions from God about what should and should not be a part of our lives. Psalm 24:3–4 (NIV) says, "Who may ascend the hill of the Lord? Who may stand in his holy place? He who has clean hands and a pure heart, who does not lift up his soul to an idol or swear by what is false." Clergy need to seek God in order to have a heart committed to him. To live the simple life is to, "trust in the Lord with all your heart and not lean to your own understanding" (Proverbs 3:5 NIV).

I can truthfully say that it is liberating, after all these years in ministry, not to be driven by personal desires (wants). I believe our personal desires get in the way and keep us from living the simple life. We can always defend our wishes by comparing our desires or our *stuff* with what other clergy have, showing that we come up on the short side of the list. However, there is no need to make comparisons, because God takes care of his own, giving us what we need. In Matthew 6:34 (NRSV) Jesus says, "So do not worry about tomorrow, for tomorrow will bring worries of its own. Today's trouble is enough for today." Maybe living the simple life was easier for those early disciples than it is for us, seeing we live in a prosperous society. However we define the "simple life" for clergy, we will surely come up with some personal sacrificing. The more we become involved with gaining material possessions, the less simple we will be living, because we will be complicating our lives with stuff that will require our time (definition 2). Ecclesiastes 7:29 (HCSB) says, "Only see this: I have discovered that God made people upright, but they pursued many schemes." The Jerusalem Bible uses the word "simple" instead of "upright." I believe God did create humans to live simple by depending on him for all their needs. We have complicated the process by inserting so many of our desires and our plans.

What are God's plans for your future? Are you seeking to know his will for your life? I believe God speaks to us in many ways about his desires for our life. It is important that we seek to understand his words to us.

CHAPTER

The Voice of God

---◆---

W hat does the voice of God sound like? That is a question many folks ask. I believe it is important to hear the voice of God and to obey what is said. The problem lies in understanding if it is the voice of God. Clergy, who seem to the public to have a more direct line to God, are no exception to wanting to know what the voice of God sounds like. Some years ago, a children's leader was gathering the children to the front of the church's sanctuary to give a children's sermon. Suddenly, one of the children asked, "What does the voice of God sound like?" The leader couldn't ignore the question, because the congregation heard it. She tried to answer by saying, "The voice of God sounds like," and nothing would come out. She tried several times without success. Finally, she gave up trying to come up with a theological answer by saying, "The voice of God might sound like your father, your mother, your brother, your sister, your teacher, your pastor, etc." This was a correct answer, because God often speaks to us through others. Some Christians have accepted that God only speaks to us through the Written Word, but I have concluded that he also speaks to us through many persons and through many circumstances.

We will do well to recall Jethro's words to his son-in-law, Moses, as recorded in the eighteenth chapter of Exodus. Moses was seeking to be faithful to God's calling by counseling with all the people about their concerns. He was wearing himself out (Exodus 18:18) by sitting from morning until night, trying to solve the people's problems. He was attempting to do more than was humanly possible. Jethro suggested that Moses choose Godly men to help him. He was to put men over groups of tens, fifties, hundreds, and thousands. I believe this was God speaking to Moses through Jethro. Thankfully, Moses accepted Jethro's advice. Clergy need friends like Jethro, who are willing to speak God's word to them. Revelation 2:7 (NIV) gives this statement: "He who has an ear, let him hear what the Spirit says to the churches." I believe this means for us to give attention to and heed God's words. I recommend that clergy listen for the voice of God daily.

I believe God has been speaking to me for quite some time about the simple life for clergy. This was confirmed when I read chapter 6 of *Celebration of Discipline,* by Richard J. Foster. The title of chapter 6 is, "The Discipline of Simplicity." Foster says, "Simplicity is freedom. Duplicity is bondage. Simplicity brings joys and balance. Duplicity brings anxiety and fear. Simplicity begins with inward focus and unity."[1] I believe I have experienced this inward focus by having a quiet time each day at the end of family devotions. I listen for the voice of God, to see what impressions come to me in my quiet time.

To achieve any lasting change in our lives, I believe we must first be focused on the reality of what the change will mean. If we do not take the time to be quiet and focus, we just might not have a clear understanding of what we should do. In the busyness of our everyday lives, we often fail to give God a chance to talk to us. God can overpower our thoughts and actions, but he doesn't usually choose to do that. He wants a willingness from us to listen to him and a respect for him that honors him with what I call "God's time." This quiet time has worked for me, as well as for my wife, Anna. It is not a time for praying but a time for just listening for the voice of God. Sometimes, God speaks to us about the scripture we have read in our devotional and sometimes about other things.

A quote from Henry David Thoreau says, "Only that day dawns to which we are awake."[2] If we have a simple life, we must first be aware of it. We must be wide-awake to the desire to live simply. It is my desire to make some noise, to be the voice of God, to stir our thoughts and emotions to action about the simple life. So many of us (clergy) know we ought to seek the simple life, but we sometimes feel overwhelmed with the amount of work that has been placed on our plate, so we put simplicity on the back burner. My desire is to awaken us once again to the necessity of giving heed to this important component of our ministries. May I speak loudly enough and with enough conviction that we not only sit up and listen, but we will begin the plan of action. Procrastination is a terrible enemy, which pursues us unceasingly. As long as a plan is in our mind and never gets set into action, it is still in the *potential* position. Having good potential is better than no potential at all, but it is better still if the potential is placed into effective action.

I recall a time when God spoke to me through the voice of a pastor friend. I was in seminary and serving as a student pastor. Sometimes, I would become depressed over the fact I was not able to do more church work than I was doing. I felt like I was not doing an adequate job with the church because of all the seminary work that was required. I tried to give the church my best effort under those circumstances, but I wanted to be full time for God. When I discussed my predicament with a clergy friend, he told me that what I was doing was honorable to God, and my position as student pastor was as important as any full-time pastor. He helped me to view that position as the place where God wanted me to be. Instead of looking at what other pastors were doing and accomplishing, with a degree of disgust with myself, I began to appreciate what God was doing through me. It helped me to stay focused.

There are so many voices calling out to us constantly in this noisy world. How can we discern the voice of God among so many? Just about the time we think we have a handle on what the voice of God sounds like, we hear other voices we think might be him. The voice of God will always be for our good; that is, it will always call us to do something good. The voice of God speaks about discipleship and about loving our neighbor as ourselves. Someone has said that we can know if God wants us to do some work by the fact that our gifts and graces cross the line (intersects) of some need, and we have a strong feeling about supplying the need. Perhaps this is one way of knowing what God wants us to do. If we have followed a calling with preparation through training/ education, God will provide instances for us to respond to the call. Don't always look for God to speak in a loud, audible voice. It might be through the still, small voice (1 Kings 19:12). Remember, it could be those impressions that come to us in our quiet time. Clergy, take time to have some quiet moments for God. It will enrich your spirituality and speak volumes to you about doing the work of God.

Maybe God does speak more to us through the Written Word. By the end of this book, you will realize the large number of biblical quotes I have given. I use them, because I believe God is directing me to do so. Clergy, it is a must for us to have a strong relationship with the Bible. God still inspires it today, over and over, as we read and study it. How often do we get new insights from it, although we have read it many times? This is one way God speaks to us. We need to take the time to get to know the Bible all over again. Only when we seek to have a close relationship with it, will it speak to us in those warm, revealing ways. Clergy need to be involved in Bible studies, even if they are not the teacher/leader. This is a great way to gain new insights into possible ministries. It also adds flavor to the sermons, especially if you are preaching them. What does the voice of God sound like? It sounds a lot like the words I read in the Bible.

It is of a surety that there is someone out there who will sooner or later seek your help or knowledge about God speaking to him or her. It is of vital spiritual importance that we answer them correctly. Prophets in the Old Testament were often mouthpieces for God. They spoke to the people (congregation/community) what God wanted them to hear. Ephesians 4:11–12 (HCSB) says, "And He personally gave some to be apostles, some prophets, some evangelists, some pastors and teachers, for the training of the saints in the work of ministry, to build up the body of Christ." This training of the saints aligns with the idea of teaching the Christians to be more mature in their Christian life. If we are to do that, we must be able to hear the voice of God speak to us. We must see ourselves as the voice of God on Sunday morning, Sunday night, Wednesday night, and in-between times. This in no way gives us the authority or right to lord it over others, as though they have no voice for God. Let us give great respect to all Christian leaders, honoring them in their work. Their voice might just be God speaking to us.

CHAPTER
3

Having Joy in Our Work

I t has been said that the majority of people in the public workforce
aren't happy in their jobs. Is that surprising? Maybe it is surprising
at times, but we often meet persons in their areas of work, and they don't
seem overjoyed with the job. We wonder why they seem so unhappy
and guess they are in the wrong field of work. Maybe that is so, but
maybe they just don't take the time to be thankful for the opportunities
they get and to see how they might be more productive in their work.
I believe we should give our best effort to whatever job we have. We
should work like we are working for ourselves, with the desire to make
ourselves proud of our work. It is important to take pride in what we
do. Even more important is that we believe we are doing the work for
God, because he has given us the ability to do it.

Clergy are no less important in their work. After all, we are seeking
to please God Almighty. It is important that we do a good job. Yet,
more than that, it is important that we are obedient to the Lord, no
matter how the results come out. God never forces us to do something
we don't want to do. If he has called us to do ministry, that is what
we should be doing and with joy in our hearts. Our real joy comes in
knowing Christ as our Savior and Lord. From this basic foundation,
we are able to build our ministries. However, I am not suggesting that
we start building on our own without the calling of God to do so. That

could produce failure and misery. If we have been in ministry for a while, we already know there are some things that can take away our joy in the work—if we let them. Just the everyday pressures of managing our schedules can be frustrating, even to the point of taking away our joy in the ministry. This is one of the "little foxes" that can spoil the vine. Sometimes, young clergy, who are brand new to their ministry, will succumb to the struggles of getting things done on time. We must learn to set priorities and know when we are in overload.

How wonderful it is for clergy to be happy in their work. It is extremely important for clergy to be satisfied with themselves. I am not talking about self-satisfaction or complacency that falls short of being all God wants us to be. I am talking about being happy with our work. It is about doing our best for God, realizing our limits, and relying on the Holy Spirit to bring results. We are called to preach, teach, nurture, and to be spiritual caregivers. We are not called to make professions of faith; that is the job of the Holy Spirit. We are called to make disciples, which involves teaching the believer. Now, just so some will not misunderstand me, let me say I fully believe we ought to pray for professions of faith and to do all we can to strengthen lives with spiritual help, so those persons will desire to make a commitment to God. However, we need to realize that the *closing of the deal* belongs to God. We don't need to put stress upon ourselves to get results. After all, we are not counting numbers, although numbers do count. We are giving ourselves to the ministry and mission of the kingdom of God. There are so many pitfalls to losing our joy in doing God's work, but we must not allow ourselves to fall into them. We must be aware of them and how to avoid them.

If we are so minded, we can allow the daily stresses of our jobs to hinder us from staying connected to our life source: the Holy Spirit. The Holy Spirit, as our life source, gives us joy, a heart of joy for doing what God has called us to do. Let us recall what Jesus said to his disciples as recorded in Matthew 6:34 (NRSV), "Therefore do not worry about tomorrow." This is not telling us to do no planning for the future, because we know we have the necessity of planning ahead or preparing. What it is saying to us is that we need not be so concerned with upcoming events or what might happen that we do not give our best to the tasks at hand. Worry tends to take away our joy. If we want to keep the joy of the Lord in our heart, we must get rid of worry. In today's busy world, it is easy to lose focus of our goals and try to keep up with some type of quota. We must remember that our goal is to stay with the *main thing*, that is, to do the work God has called us to do, whatever else is happening around us.

In his book, *My Utmost for His Highest*, Oswald Chambers asks the question, Is He Really Lord? Under this heading, he talks about receiving a ministry from the Lord. He says:

> Joy means the perfect fulfillment of that for which I was created and regenerated, not the successful doing of a thing. The joy Our Lord had lay in doing what the Father sent him to do, and He says—"As My Father hath sent Me, even so am I sending you." Have I received a ministry from the Lord? If so, I have to be loyal to it, to count my life precious only for the fulfilling of that ministry … We have all to find our niche in life, and spiritually we find it when we receive our ministry from the Lord. In order to do this we must have companied with Jesus; we must know Him as more than a personal Saviour. "I will show him how great things he must suffer for my sake."[3]

So, we know that the joy of the Lord for clergy, as well as for laity, comes in our fulfilling of what God has called us to do. We have been called to present the gospel of Christ to others, seeking to lead them to Christ. To continue in our joy, we must continue to do that for which we have been called. Leading someone to commit his or her life to Christ is not an overnight experience. There are often many steps in building that house. It takes a great deal of commitment from the person who wishes to lead others into the service of the Lord. Having a disciplined life is most important, before we attempt to get others to be disciplined. Living the simple life involves knowing we do not possess the power or intellect to convince someone automatically to commit his or her life to Christ. However, we know we belong to the One who called us to this ministry, and we can offer him all we have and all we are. I say all this to say that clergy can give in to impatience and a lack of long suffering, therefore losing focus of their purpose and, in turn, losing their joy in doing God's work. The latter part of Nehemiah 8:10

(KJV) says, "for the joy of the Lord is your strength." We can stay strong in the Lord if we keep our joy, and our joy is in doing what God has called us to do. I believe it is so important for us to have the joy of the Lord in our work, that we should not let anything impede our gaining it and keeping it.

In order to keep the joy in our work as clergy, we must allow ourselves to be refreshed from time to time. We need little sabbaticals to keep our focus. We need time off every so often to refresh ourselves. This time away from work could be a trip to the mountains, the ocean, or visiting other special sites. It could be a weekend seminar covering some subject related to doing ministry effectively. I recall that during a stressful time in my pastoral ministry, I signed up for Feeding the Shepherd, a three-day retreat in the mountains of North Carolina. This retreat was a most relaxing event. It was so wonderful that I signed up for it the next year. I was taught that as pastor, I needed to take time off work, at least one day a week, and not feel guilty about it. The shepherd (under-shepherds) sometimes needs refueling. There are many helpful things (retreats, seminars, convocations, small group studies, reading a new book, joining a prayer group, etc.) clergy can do to keep the joy in their work. We have to find what works for us at the needed time. For example, if we are having problems with managing our time, we might want to sign up for a time management class. If we are struggling with stress, we might want to take a class or go to a retreat that teaches us to relax. What I am saying is that keeping the joy of the Lord in our life is important enough to do whatever it takes to keep it. Without it, our ministries will fail. If, as Nehemiah 8:10 (KJV) says, "the joy of the Lord is our strength," then *w*ithout it, we are powerless.

Sometimes, clergy find themselves in a faraway place, trying to do ministry. Maybe this ministry is set in the mountains or far out in the country, away from the city or populated areas. Perhaps it is a place that doesn't have much to offer in outside activities, such as a library, playground, ball field, running/walking track, or bookstore. Maybe you are an intellectual type or an academician. What are you to do to keep yourself (body, mind) in good working order? This is a part of keeping the joy of the Lord in our work. Well, we might try contacting fellow clergy (if any are close enough to where we live) to see if they have any suggestions about other places that would offer help with what we are seeking. I have a background in theology, so at one time in my ministry, I joined three other fellow clergy for what we called "Theological Thursdays." It was a two-hour session each Thursday, where we could discuss various theological issues. This served to keep my mind fresh on particular religious or theological subjects. I believe this was a catalyst that served to boost joy in my ministry. It certainly fed my theological intellect. It kept me connected to the main thing.

I have heard it said that we never get a second chance to make a first impression. I think about this often. Do our facial expressions, actions, and body language exhibit an image of joy in our work to those persons we meet for the first time? We shouldn't put on a false expression or give a false impression of who we are or how we feel about our work. The truth is, if we have pure joy in our work as clergy, it will come through without much effort on our part. When I was preparing for pastoral ministry, I interviewed some clergy. I shall never forget my interview with one pastor. His demeanor was such that I could see, right from the start of the interview, that he was happy (joyful) in his work. Actually, before the interview was over, he told me he could not imagine doing anything else. That interview helped me so often in trying times of my ministry. Having *joy* in our work is the key to having a successful or continuing ministry.

Clergy will have many trying moments: those times when we wonder if staying in ministry is worth it. Is it worth all the hassles, times of disrespect, persecutions, long hours, attempts to please everyone, and pure exhaustion? I am not trying to be pessimistic here. I am just reminding us that the real joy of the Lord will get us through those times. We cannot manufacture this joy on our own. Sure, we can do specific things that will keep us happy for a while, but doing what God wants us to do will bring the pure, unadulterated joy. The simple life for clergy involves our dependence on God to give us joy rather than on our attempts to bring it about. Let me explain. As I have shown in some examples, there are things we can do to enhance our joy in God's work, but we recognize that God is guiding us to do them. I believe God has chosen to speak to us through various media about our commitment to him. I do believe that God is speaking through me to give you these exhortations about your ministry. My prayer is that I not be too presumptuous about any of this. I feel strongly that what God has given me is worthy of putting into the written word. There are far too many clergy who do not exhibit joy in their work and yet as many who live defeated lives. We need to take a stand against our spiritual enemy, expressing loudly and clearly that our joy is *not for sale*. It is not up for grabs. May it be too valuable to us, for us to ever take a chance on losing it. May it be to us what Psalm 119:11 (HCSB) says about God's word: "I have treasured Your word in my heart so that I may not sin against You." Psalm 119:105 (HCSB) says, "Your word is a lamp for my feet and a light on my path." If we can be so sure about the *joy* of the Lord as the psalmist is about God's Word, we will have no problem living the simple life.

In seeking to live the simple life, with the joy of the Lord as our encourager, we need to meditate on and obey the following words from a poem in *Good Morning Lord: Meditations for Modern Marrieds* by Louis O. Caldwell:

Every morning, lean thine arms awhile
Upon the windowsill of heaven,
And gaze upon the Lord...
Then with that vision in thy heart,
Turn strong to meet the day.[4]

In order to keep the joy in our work for God, we must begin each day with renewal in our spirit from the Spirit. It is my hope that each clergy reading this will commit to seeking God early each day, instead of rushing off in a dash to keep up with a demanding itinerary. Remember what I said earlier about *God's time*: allow God to speak to you early each morning, so you can be sure to follow his orders. Doing what God wants you to do each day will surely bring you joy, no matter what the day entails. We might miss the mark of doing what God wants us to do if we don't start off each day with prayer and meditation. It is important that we allow God to speak to our heart each morning, before we attempt to engage in our daily schedules. Feeling the warmth of the Holy Spirit and knowing that we are under the guiding light of God can give us confidence in our work and help us maintain our joy.

Chapter

Clergy and Wealth

———————— ✦ ————————

C lergy need to examine their lives constantly to see if they are keeping Christ the number-one priority. In this day of wealth and vast resources, we can quickly be overcome with desires to gain riches and status for ourselves. First John 4:1 (Amplified Bible) says, "Beloved, Do not put faith in every spirit, but prove the spirits to discover whether they proceed from God; for many false prophets have gone forth into the world." We need to be careful to check out every spirit (desire or motivation) in order to know if God is leading us. Socrates, the great Greek philosopher, said that the *unexamined* life was not worth living. There is a lot of truth in that statement. How often do we examine our lives? What if we find, on examination, that we are too greedy or too interested in gaining wealth? What do we do? First, we repent of our greed. Next, we find constructive work to do, like supporting a food bank or donating money to a homeless shelter. Of course, just because we might be a little too greedy doesn't mean we have much money. We might just have the spirit of greed by constantly fantasizing about wealth. But if we have an abundance of money, we can use it wisely to care for others.

Not many clergy that I know are wealthy. Most of them fare quite well, though. We should never desire a larger parish in order to gain more money that will be used on our selfish desires. The more we gain monetarily, the more we will be able to contribute to the ministry and missions of God. Some clergy live in abundant wealth, while other clergy struggle to provide for their families. My focus is not to make comparisons between clergy and their amount of income, but I believe that gaining more money can be obsessive. Clergy should be in love with giving! We can give of our time, our gifts, and graces, and yes, our money. I have gotten the impression from some clergy that they do not need to give much money to the church's missions, because they are giving their time in ministry. While most of us might not have much money to give, we should set the example in proportionate giving.

John Wesley's sermon "The Danger of Riches" has been very inspirational to me. It was written over two hundred years ago, but it still evokes much thought about what riches do to the receiver. Wesley often wrote to the clergy who served under him. In this sermon, he writes in rather bold fashion:

> Herein, my brethren, let you that are rich be even as I am. Do you that possess more than food and raiment ask: What shall we do? Shall we throw into the sea what God hath given us? God forbid that you should! It is an excellent talent: It may be employed much to the glory of God. Your way lies plain before your face; If you have courage, walk in it. Having gained (in a right sense) all you can, and saved all you can; in spite of nature, and custom, and worldly prudence, give all you can. I do not say, Be a good Jew, giving a tenth of all you possess. I do not say, Be a good Pharisee, giving a fifth of all your substance. I dare not advise you to give half of what you have; no, nor three-quarters—but all! Lift up your hearts and you will see clearly in what sense this is to be done.[5]

Wesley cared so much for the poor people of England that he prepared inexpensive tracts for them to read. These tracts sold so well that Wesley generated quite a bit of money. He did not lay up the treasure for himself but gave it to the work of helping those in need. He did not wish to die and leave behind an abundance of riches. He got his wish. When he died, he hardly had anything that was worth mentioning except his books and, of course, the great spiritual legacy he left behind. I can hardly expect today's clergy to measure up to Wesley or to try and copy him, but we can use his life as an example and inspiration. I do believe in his principles. What he taught was for every Christian, especially Methodists. What I propose is for clergy, regardless of denomination. Wesley believed that God-called preachers had no time to gather wealth to themselves. Things have changed a lot since Wesley's time (1700s), but today's clergy will do well to heed the words of that wise one.

Richard Foster quoting Søren Kierkegaard says:

" ... riches and abundance come physically clad in sheep's clothing pretending to be security against anxieties and they become then the object of anxiety ... they secure a man against anxieties just about as well as the wolf which is put to tending the sheep secures them ... against the wolf."[6]

It is true that possessions of wealth can cause anxieties. We need money to live, but accumulating an abundance of it can cause problems for clergy. It seems there are always persons who are trying to gain more income for various reasons. They are quite anxious about it and spend an unusual amount of time trying to get it. Clergy can fall into the same trap. A lot of our time can be spent seeking more wealth, while our ministry lies in waste. We can become addicted to gaining more. We might see ourselves far below our deserved income levels and decide we need to do something to gain more. It is important that we budget ourselves according to our income and learn to live within our means. I am not saying there are not times when someone (perhaps the local church) needs to consider giving the clergy a raise. This is always helpful and should be appreciated. However, if we spend a lot of time worrying over our income, we will cause a great deal of stress that might possibly interfere with our duties. Anxiety will build up, and we can experience health difficulties from it. Anxiety has a way of controlling our thoughts and decisions. Freedom from undue anxiety should be a goal of every clergy. If our priorities are in order—God, others, and self—we will see anxiety diminish. Of course, we are talking about clergy and wealth, not about simple anxiety. If our thoughts are always dollar signs, we are in trouble.

There are many temptations for clergy to gather wealth and material goods. Only those who focus deeply on Christ and his will for them are able to overcome the subtle temptations. I truly like the finer things of life and do not judge those who have an abundance of them. For me, I know that I must discipline myself to enjoy what God has provided for me and not spend time wishing for more. When the evil monster of greed has caught hold, it is hard to shake loose. As clergy, we are often tempted to maintain certain social levels of life in order to be accepted by so-called elite groups. I enjoy having friends at all socioeconomic levels, but if my acceptance depends on wealth, I can do without the wealthy elite friends.

Living the simple life doesn't mean we have to be poor, but it certainly has the element of not becoming rich built into it. It does mean that we do not have time to go seeking wealth, because we have committed our life to Christ. It is quite tempting to want to be like our workaholic neighbors when we see them buy new automobiles, RVs, boats, and even new furniture. We begin to think that if we could just find one more job, we could make enough money to do some of those things. Now, don't take me wrong; I don't believe clergy have to live in poverty. In fact, in today's prosperous world, most of us can live quite well as clergy. We just don't need to have thoughts of making money high on our list. If we become wealthy by some means other than our own (it is unlikely), we can have a wonderful ministry to the poor!

My intention is not to persuade clergy that prosperity is sinful but to affirm the role of clergy in living the simple life, so they will have satisfaction in ministry and success in persuading others to seek Christ. In 3 John 2 (KJV), there is a verse we like to quote often. It says, "Beloved, I wish above all things that thou mayest prosper and be in health, even as thy soul prospereth." Too often, we think of prosperity as wealth. I don't believe John was referring to wealth (money) in this scripture. The word "prospereth" has reference to spiritual well-being. If we read verse 3, we will see that John is rejoicing that Gaius is walking in the truth. This walking in the truth makes one spiritually wealthy. Prospering in Christ means going forward spiritually, maturing in the faith. That is my desire for clergy. I wish that all of us might prosper spiritually, so we, in turn, can share with others.

Richard Foster says that because we lack a divine Center, we have a need for security, which leads us into an insane attachment to things. He calls society's lust for affluence "psychotic." He says:

> This psychosis permeates even our mythology. The modern hero is the poor boy who purposefully becomes rich rather than the rich boy who voluntarily becomes poor … Covetousness we call ambition. Hoarding we call prudence. Greed we call industry.[7]

It is easy to redefine our understanding of covetousness, hoarding, and greed in a society that constantly challenges us to gain more. Especially in stressful economic times, we are tempted to build our little empires for our security in the future. We must be careful not to give new definitions to old words, which speak about things as they are. Society might attempt to stamp us with new ideas about wealth, but in Christ, we will know the difference. What is our spiritual conscience (the inner person who speaks to us after the mind of Christ) telling us? The inner voice of the Spirit will speak the truth to us. We need to listen carefully.

Happiness and contentment do not come with having more but with learning to live with less. Hebrews 13:5 (NIV) says, "Keep yourselves free from the love of money and be content with what you have, because God has said, 'Never will I leave you; never will I forsake you.'" There is freedom in wanting less wealth or material goods. If we can discipline ourselves to want less, we will be free to do God's work. Howard Rice speaks about clergy breaking free from bondage:

> We need to be free to follow the leading of the Holy Spirit into the unknown future. May that divine power free us from our various forms of slavery and set us on the road to a form of pastoral ministry that is rooted and grounded in Christ's powerful love.[8]

Clergy can become slaves to various forms of materialism. One of these forms is gaining more wealth. It can be a terrible addiction. It can become easy to follow the course set by others rather than cut a path by our own commitment and desire to follow God's instructions. Ministry is never more fulfilling than when we break free from the hindrances that bind us and keep us from being spiritually productive. Trying to keep up with the economic resources of our neighbors and friends can destroy our well-being. To those who are totally committed to serving Christ, material things become just *stuff*. Stuff often clutters and gets in our way. We need to break free from the desire to get more stuff. We are not called to be rich, except to be spiritually rich in Christ.

In Matthew 6, we see that Jesus told his disciples they were not to worry over their needs, because God, the Father, knew what their needs were. He instructed them to seek the kingdom of God first, and then their needs would be supplied. How are we doing in trusting Christ to take care of our needs? Are we constantly complaining about not having enough, or are we daily giving God thanks for supplying our needs? In Philippians 4:19 (KJV), Paul says to the Philippian Christians, "But my God shall supply all your need according to his riches in glory by Christ Jesus." Clergy need to commit this scripture to memory and recite it often to themselves. Living the simple life means we will trust Christ with all our needs. He wants to have the opportunity to do good for us. Perhaps we often get so independently minded that we try doing it all on our own. What happens then? Many of us, no doubt, remember times when we became frustrated with our failed efforts. When we submitted to the Lord and got back to the real work of ministry, things worked out. I could tell you of a number of times when the Lord supplied my family's needs most bountifully. For some folks, this trusting in God to take care of us is the lazy or slothful way. They think God only helps those who help themselves. I am strongly aware that God even helps those who cannot help themselves.

Maybe there is a fine line between what God calls us to do to help ourselves and what God does for us when we cannot help ourselves. I am aware that not all clergy are full time in ministry. There are many bi-vocational clergy. These clergy seek employment outside the church in order to take care of themselves and their families. This is understandable. They give as much time as possible in public ministry. God honors all our commitments in various forms of ministry. It is when we take away from our committed ministry time—to seek material wealth—that we are displeasing to God. Most clergy have some stories to tell about how God miraculously supplied their needs. This is God's plan. This is the way he does things. No, it is not the secular way, but it is God's way. Remember, the scripture warns us that we cannot serve God and mammon (money). When clergy put their thoughts too heavily on wealth, their ministry suffers. It mentally and physically takes us away from our called duties.

Speaking to the Christians at Philippi (Philippians 4:12-13, HCSB), Paul says, "I know both how to have a little, and I know how to have a lot. In any and all circumstances I have learned the secret of being content whether well fed or hungry, whether in abundance or in need. I am able to do all things through him who strengthens me. " Can we clergy say the same thing with him? Are we willing to continue to work for God no matter what the circumstances? Do we believe we have been called and sent by Christ and that he can help us do whatever we need to do? From the scriptures, it seems like God calls us to be totally reliant on him to supply our needs, without us seeking the extra load that comes with more wealth.

My wife and I had some financial investments a few years ago, and the stock market dropped drastically. We were saving for our retirement years. The loss of money was a great concern for us. We were not a part of the fortunate few who started saving early in life, so we had to work harder to provide for our retirement. I know God wants us to be wise in our earthly tasks, even in our investments, but somewhere in the scheme of things concerning our loss, I received consolation from God that all was not lost. God has a way of teaching us special things right in the middle of our discouragement. If we put too much trust in our own plans, we might possibly be in for a great deal of disappointment. If we allow God to guide us, he will often surprise us with his miraculous way of doing things. I am thankful to God that I unloaded on him and allowed him to free me from worrying about the financial loss. After all, he did not call me to build a future on financial grounds solely, but primarily on his providence. Another way of saying this is that God has called us to a faith in him—not one in ourselves. However, he does give us confidence to do many things, and because of our faith in him, we accomplish them.

CHAPTER

5

Meeting the World

H ow do we meet the world as God-called preachers? How
do we present ourselves to those to whom we are called to
minister? Is it with arrogance and pride, or is it with humbleness and
sincerity? We can allow our titles to get in the way of humbly walking
into someone's life, or we can go in as the called servants of God. (I will
say more about servants in chapter 7.) How we enter another's life will
make a difference in how we conduct ourselves as clergy on a mission
to help someone. How do we see ourselves? Do we see ourselves cast
into a sea of needs without a boat, or do we see the opportunity to be
God's voice to someone calling out for help? There are so many needs
out there. People are hurting for various reasons and need a balm to
ease the pain. Clergy cannot be all things to all people at all times, but
we can be there with our willingness to help. Just showing love and
concern is a big help. Persons need to know that they count; that is, they
are an important part of this earth. Every living creature is important
to God. We clergy are the messengers sent from God to encourage and
strengthen the faith of all who will receive us.

How do we see those who are in need? Do we see them as worthy
of God's attention through us? Without people who have needs, you
and I would not stay in business. We would not have any clients. Our
business—God's business—would be a failure. In her book *Don't Put*

a Period Where God Put a Comma, Nell W. Mohney writes about the power of expectation. She speaks about how our expectations influence others. She asks these questions:

> How am I limiting my God-given potential? By critical self talk? By fear of failure? By unwillingness to try something new? By unwillingness to be specific in listing expectations? Who are the people in my life I am limiting through low expectations, criticism, sarcasm, gossip, or by ignoring them?[9]

Although her book is not specifically for clergy, these questions are pertinent to us. Clergy need to ask themselves if they are limiting their God-given potentials. We must learn to *unlimit* ourselves. We need to understand that God can give us all the resources necessary to be successful for him. In fact, he *does* give us all we need to get the job done. This success, understandably, is not that of worldly success, which involves a great deal of recognition by means of various media, but it is the success of building the kingdom of God by gaining people to Christ. When we realize we are not in competition with anyone, except to oppose the powers of evil, we will be able to have the freedom to obey God and to know that through the strength of Christ, we can do all the things he wants us to do. To live the simple life is to see others as equals. We will see them as creatures of God Almighty, created to be the best they can be for him. It is possible that clergy can limit people by their low expectations of them, criticizing them, through sarcasm and gossip, or by ignoring them. Clergy are expected to be positive and uplifting to persons. The world is full of troubles and heartaches. We need to be there to tell the lowly in heart and spirit that tomorrow can be better. When we expect God to listen attentively to our prayers and to send us beneficial answers, we can offer hope to others. If we have any baggage of unbelief, we need to seek God with all our heart to get rid of it.

Several years ago, I served as chaplain of the local Optimist Club. The Optimist Club seeks to be *a* friend of youth and help them have an optimistic outlook for the future. I have often received strength and inspiration from reading and meditating on the Optimist Creed, which says:

Promise Yourself. To be so strong that nothing can disturb your peace of mind. To talk health, happiness and prosperity to every person you meet. To make all your friends feel that there is something in them. To look at the sunny side of everything and make your optimism come true. To think only of the best, to work only for the best and expect only the best. To be just as enthusiastic about the success of others as you are about your own. To forget the mistakes of the past and press on to greater achievements of the future. To wear a cheerful countenance at all times and give every living creature you meet a smile. To give so much time to the improvement of yourself that you have no time to criticize others. To be too large for worry, too noble for anger, too strong for fear, and too happy to permit the presence of trouble.[10]

Now, that sounds like an impossible way to live, seeing that we encounter so many difficulties every day. Yet, doesn't it sound a lot like it comes from the Bible? If we put various passages of scripture together, it could sound similar to the above creed. Maybe the originator of it was greatly influenced by the Bible. Maybe he or she saw the positivism or optimism from the biblical writers about living out the Christian life. At any rate, if a secular club can have guidelines like that, surely we, leaders in Christ's church, can be disciplined as much. Clergy will do well to keep a copy of this creed with them at all times, reading it often and applying it to their everyday journey in ministry. What would the world be like if everyone put these principles into practice? Now, we know that everyone is not going to do that, but we can be rest assured that if all of us that read the Optimist Creed, pass it on to others, and seek to apply it to our everyday life, this world will not be the same.

Mother Teresa was asked why she committed her life to helping the indigent in India, seeing that she was only helping a small part of the world's population. She replied that her little portion helped those who received from her. I heard another story once that impressed me and gave me inspiration to do what I can, where I can. This young boy was picking up starfish and throwing them back into the ocean, knowing they would die if left on the hot sand. When someone asked him what difference it made, seeing that there were so many starfish on the beach, he reached down, picked up a starfish, and flung it back into the ocean. He replied, "It made a difference to that one!" May we, God's ambassadors, be intentional about how we present ourselves to those who are in need. Every person counts. Every person matters. Every person in need whom we are called to help should be made to feel they are our priority for the day. The simple life calls us to do what seems to the world to be *too* simple. The little things count—big time.

I have heard that on our journey of life, if we have at least two good friends—that is, the kind of friends we could share anything with and they would still be our friends—we are doing great. With that thought in mind, shouldn't clergy be that type of friend with others in whom they can have confidence? Shouldn't we be so committed to God and his mission that we would make those in need feel like they have hope and a bright future? Only if we are full of optimism (I call it faith), will we be able to help them have courage to face tomorrow. How does the world see us? Are we ready to judge those who have been caught up in sinful practices, who are hurting viciously, or are we willing to suffer alongside them and cradle them in our warm hearts of caring? Who among us has not sinned? Let that one cast the first stone! My heart often breaks when I hear someone put down one who has fallen to the enemy's temptations. I wonder if the critical one has lifted them up in prayer. It does make a difference how we, clergy, meet the world. Remember, we won't get the second chance to make the first impression.

I suppose all this puts a lot of pressure on us to do what sometimes seems impossible. The simple life doesn't call us to be perfect, but it does call us to be committed to what God has called us. Only God knows what *perfect* is. He will guide us toward perfection if we set our hearts on doing his will. It is not a game for clergy to see how much more perfect we can be than our fellow clergy. It is a call to do our best for God in the process of loving our neighbor. We need to enter every day with a humble spirit about what we can do and about how little we can do on our own, without the help of the Holy Spirit. Let us recall what Nell Mohney said in the title of her book *Don't Put a Period Where God Put a Comma*. We must keep open our lines of communication with heaven. We must have great expectations of the Holy Spirit. He can help us to do all things Christ has called us to do.

One way I remember a person's name is to repeat it after he or she is introduced to me. For example, if I am introduced to Bob Smith, I say, "Bob, I am pleased to meet you." Something about repeating the name helps me remember them. I suppose our brains download or process the information for later use. By the same token, what do clergy do to recall who it is that we are supposed to help (visit with, pray for, read the Bible to, or just give encouragement to)? Now, I am well aware that we usually write ourselves notes, putting them in conspicuous places, and have itineraries that give us direction for each day's schedule. But do we go to pray for someone and then feel like we have done our job? Or do we continue to pray for them and then visit with them to see if we can be of further help? Most of all, we should have them in our heart (mind), so we do not forget their needs. How serious are we about bringing healing to someone? Healing is not always an instantaneous, getting well physically process. Healing is a process for the mind, soul (psyche), and body. The only sure way that we can talk convincingly about healing is if we have experienced it ourselves. Clergy need to communicate with God in a serious manner about any healing we need. After all, many of those who request our prayers feel like they have given their needs to God. In the real sense, they have, if we truthfully represent him.

So, what difference does it make if we smile at the cashier at the local grocery, giving her (him) a kind word, or not speaking at all and not looking at the person? I believe it makes all the difference in the world. It might indicate how we feel about approaching those who are in need. I know some of you are asking what a situation like this has to do with ministry, but I believe it makes a difference how we see all persons. Every person is a creation of God and deserves to be respected for being a human. If we are not going to give our best to the hurting people of the world, we ought to stay away from them. I often talk about *being Christian on purpose.* What I mean is that we should go forth each day with the intention of being ready to help anyone we meet, who is in need. Of course, this does not mean that we hand out money on the corner to everyone with an outstretched hand who comes along. But how often do we miss the outstretched heart of those who are begging for someone to show them the way home? I often feel guilty that I have passed by those in need without offering to help. Now, this might not seem *simple* at all to some of you. It might seem strange and complicated. My desire has been to encourage us to be truehearted about our ministries, so we can be totally obedient to God.

There is a story of a bishop who would get up from bed and dress fully before going to prayer when a special need would come in, even if it were in the middle of the night. Someone finally asked the bishop why he did that. His answer was that he was coming into the presence of the King. That sounds a little ridiculous to some of us, but we have to honor the bishop for his feelings. He was well aware of who God is and how he deserves to be honored. We can learn a lesson from this story. Clergy should seek to stay spiritually dressed in our robes of righteousness. How we meet the world does matter, and how we approach God, for the world, matters. If we are to come boldly before the throne of grace, we must have on all the spiritual dress with which God has supplied us.

Now, once again, I urge us to be humble about our status as clergy. Some of us have a long list of credentials, either from the church or from educational institutions, and maybe from both. These will do a lot to advance us in the hierarchy of the church if we are on that route. But I suggest that we give God all the glory for the good things we have been taught, and seek to use them in a most humble and modest manner. The main thing is to keep our heart right with God, and he will promote us as he wishes. We just need to remember that we should make sure that our heart is filled every day with love for those who are hurting in this world of sin before we make any attempt to do ministry. When we see the drunk on the street, the drug addict in some type of hyperactivity, or the prostitute on the corner, can we say, "Except for the grace of God, there I go"? It is a heavy burden to carry sometimes, caring for the sin-infested ones; the ones who abuse themselves with drugs, alcohol, and illicit sex; and those who are always engaged in some illegal activity. But in each generation, life has always presented those types of persons. The good news is that a deliverer has come and is waiting to set them free from their bondage! My prayer is that we, the clergy, will allow the Holy Spirit to direct us in how we meet them.

CHAPTER

Having a Heart for Ministry

———————— ✦ ————————

Living the simple life can provide clergy with the means of keeping the main thing, the main thing. The main thing is for us to be able to present Christ to the world and to pray for transformation in human lives. We must be filled with energy from the Holy Spirit in order to keep on giving. Our lives must be ordered after the Holy Spirit for us to do what is beneficial for God. In his book *A Work of Heart*, Reggie McNeal demonstrates how God shapes the leader's heart. He says:

> Spiritual leadership needs to be competent. Spiritual leaders must develop their microskills to the fullest capacity. They must understand leadership dynamics and organizational dynamics and family systems dynamics … They must know what needs doing. Bringing the best skills and energy to bear on something that is not worth doing is a waste of time, of people, and of leadership.[11]

McNeal knows all too well that leaders who refuse to let God change their heart will end up in burnout, have a ministry that is not satisfying, and often have spiritual shipwreck. The happiest clergy I see are those who know, without a doubt, they are where God wants them to be and doing what God wants them to do. I do not believe it is difficult to know what God wants us to do. We have to learn to listen to God and to discern his voice from the many voices we hear. We have to listen for his voice in the midst of the others.

I have seen some clergy who had a heart for ministry and others who seemed to dread the everyday commitment. I still believe that God personally calls us to specific ministries. Only when we have a heart to serve God and a commitment of our life to him can we actually have a heart for ministry. I don't believe Christian ministry is a *vocation* to choose on our own but, rather, a calling to live out. There are arguments for the vocation side, and I would never try to dissuade anyone from the work of ministry, but I believe that God can change our heart and give us the calling we need. As an old cliché says, if anything is worth doing, it is worth doing right. Ministry is worth doing, and we need a heart for it in order to do it right. Now, to be sure you understand me, I am *not* saying there is a set rule(s) for doing ministry, but I am saying that to do it right (the way God wishes), we must have our heart set on it, without wavering. If our heart is not in it, it will not last. Having a heart for ministry will withstand the hard times: the times when we fumble and even the times of persecution. If our heart is not in our ministry, we ought to pray for God to give us a heart for it.

But what does it really mean to have a heart for ministry? I believe it means that no matter what, we still want to do our ministry for God. We don't really want to quit when those tempting times to walk away come to us. For a short time, we are blinded to the joy of our work by the excessively heavy workload, the inability to make the parishioners happy, and the need for a break. Yet, when all is said and done, if our heart is in it, we still feel the calling. Early in my days of ministry, I had a teacher who said we could know for sure that we were called by God if, after what we considered a miserable failure at preaching a sermon, we still had the "go ye" spirit. I believe what he was saying was, when we don't feel like we can do it, but something inside us says, "Keep going," we need to grab on, dig in, and do it. We will have many disappointing times in ministry, but God didn't tell us it would all be sunshine. Our attitude will make a world of difference. We can have an enduring attitude if our heart is in it. We must remember that our spiritual enemy will keep telling us we might as well give up, because we cannot win. Our answer to him can be that this spirit inside us will keep fighting for the right. We know that our spirit is guided by the Spirit.

Many clergy face burnout at some point on their journey of ministry. Burnout is a misunderstood expression. In order to have real burnout, one has to have faced some extremely difficult situations over an extended period of time. Clergy can become exhausted with the many chores in ministry. Exhaustion can be fixed with a little rearranging. Burnout is not that easy to fix. It involves physical, emotional, and psychological stresses. It is important that clergy take care of themselves spiritually. If we have a heart for ministry, we will make sure we are refilled from time to time. We cannot go on without some refreshing in our spirit. It is important that clergy think positively. It is the practice of having faith. It is believing that God cares and will answer our prayers. It is knowing that we will not do everything perfectly but that we have second chances. If we set our hearts to obey God in all things and know that it is only by the Holy Spirit's help that we can overcome, we will be able to face the challenges and be victorious.

Second Corinthians 5:18 tells us that we have received the ministry of reconciliation. How can we reconcile others to God if we are not reconciled to him? If we have somehow lost our earnest desire to please the Lord with our life and ministry, we should find a quiet place, and spend some time with him in prayer to be renewed in him. We will know if we have a heart for ministry or not by how we feel about going to work each morning. If we are eager to get started each day, it sounds like our heart is in it. But if we can think of a bunch of things we would rather be doing, we might want to question our heart. If we are risen with Christ, we should represent him as the Resurrected One, who gives new life to those who call on him. Leonardo Boff speaks of the shape of a resurrected life. In answering his question, What would a raised, a resurrected life be like? he tells us that a resurrected life is a *full* life and that we reach our fullness of life in the expression and activation of our latent dynamisms. The basic dynamism of life, he expresses, is the mutual exchange of giving and receiving of communion.[12] Boff, a liberation theologian in Latin America, knows about the simple life, especially about one that is forced on people, including the clergy. The clergy in that part of the world probably will have no need to read my book about living the simple life, seeing that they are already living much of what I say.

I like the idea of living a resurrected life in Christ. If we are resurrected with Christ, our message about him will come from a heart renewed in him. We must know firsthand what *new life* in Christ means. Nicodemus, a member of the Jewish Sanhedrin Court, questioned Jesus about the new life (being born again). Jesus told him that he shouldn't marvel (be surprised) about it. Jesus questioned how Nicodemus, a master (ruler) in Israel, wouldn't know about the new life (John 3:1–10 KJV). Various clergy use different terms to describe our experience in Christ. Some of us use words like "born again," "born from above," "saved," "profession of faith," and "delivered from bondage." Whatever words we use, they need to convey a *regenerated heart*. Having a new life in Christ (resurrected life) means that we can have a heart for ministry, which will allow us to be in communion with others and with the Holy Spirit. If we are going to be able to identify with, and care for, those persons hurting and in need, we need a heart committed to loving them. Jesus had compassion for persons in need. The Gospels tell us of many times when Jesus reached out a helping hand to those in desperate need. Clergy ought to pray for compassion like Jesus had when he walked upon the earth.

Clergy should not measure their commitment (or lack of it) by that of someone else—except Jesus. If we do, and that someone else doesn't have a heart for ministry, we might find ourselves coming up short. We need to have our own understanding of what it means to be committed to Christ. Now, that doesn't mean it is totally up to us to decide what the standard should be. But it is up to us to set our heart on doing God's will. Not all clergy are in the same type of ministry, so our actions of commitment will be different. We need to know that being committed to working long hours doesn't necessarily mean our heart is in it. Now, that might take some explaining. What I mean is this: long hours away from home might mean we are not happy at home (may that not happen). It could mean we are trying to impress a superior (God forbid). It could mean we are trying to make up for wasted time. It could mean a lot of things. The best answer would be that our heart is so tuned to God that we are full of compassion for those in need. Of course, you recall me talking about exhaustion and burnout. We need to be careful about that.

If our heart is truly in our ministry, we will seek God for knowledge about our schedules. Some clergy take off two days a week, while others take only one day, and some won't take off even one day. There are various views from clergy about that, and I don't propose to make any suggestions here, except to say we must be cautious about our health and do the wise thing. My greatest concern is that our heart be in our work to the point where we cannot see ourselves doing anything else. That is not limiting us; it is asking for commitment for the long haul. If the world (people of the world) has a change of heart, we must lead the way by example. I might not be the recognized expert in all areas in which I seek to help other clergy, but I believe my years of experience in ministry has taught me a lot that I need to pass on as encouragement. One thing I have learned, without a doubt, is if our heart is not in it, we are going to fail. For clergy, living the simple life means we are going to trust our hearts to God through Jesus Christ. We are not going to complicate matters by trying to do our own thing, our own way.

Jeremiah 3:15 (KJV) says, "And I will give you pastors according to mine heart, which shall feed you with knowledge and understanding." As long as I was a pastor, I believe I had a pastor's heart. Because of this, I was required to make some sacrifices. I didn't regret making the sacrifices, though. I enjoyed the pastoral caregiving, along with the preaching and teaching. My heart was committed to showing the love of God to the people. This is not meant to be a brag session for me, only my way of showing that ministry (pastoral, in my case) can be most enjoyable. I believe that my parishioners saw the joy in my life. I desired them to see it, so they would know my heart was in it. My desire was to give people knowledge and understanding about living an effective Christian life. I tried to teach in simple terms what it means to be a disciplined Christian. I worked hard to translate seminary language into lay language. I believe this is part of the simple life for clergy.

CHAPTER

Being a Servant

———————— ✧ ————————

To live the simple life means we understand we have not *arrived* yet, but we are ever *becoming.* We will not be prideful about accomplishing so much or gaining so much, but we will seek to understand more, to know more, and to do more. We have plenty of room to expand our knowledge and understanding.

We can give credit to the understanding of becoming to Alfred North Whitehead, mathematician, scientist, and philosopher. At Harvard University in the 1920s, Whitehead described reality as a process of becoming. Out of this understanding and vision came process theology. Process theology has been combined with pastoral care to bring knowledge to pastoral caregivers about helping persons become people of beauty and wholeness.[13] I believe persons are constantly seeking to improve areas of their lives. Clergy can be a means of grace that inspires them to reach for a handle on that change.

I say this to let you know that clergy are to be servants. It is our job to serve others. We are to help them to be all they can be. A servant doesn't always get recognition for his or her work. A servant's job is a lowly one. A servant takes orders from someone and seeks to please the master. The words "servant" and "slave" come from the same root. The Greek word *doulos* means servant or slave. We don't like the word "slave" very much because it has connotations about forced work. We think a servant may be a hired worker. However, a servant is someone who is committed to serving the needs of someone else. The servant does what will make the master (boss) look good. As Christian servants, clergy seek to bring honor and glory to our master (Christ). The Apostle Paul referred to himself as a servant (slave) to Christ. He wanted to give the proper identification of who he was: a child of God. He described himself as freely being a slave to Christ. Can we, clergy, see ourselves voluntarily being servants to Christ, which means that we freely serve others? Can we serve without dollar signs in our eyes? It is good that we can make a living from our ministries (some Christians don't believe we should), but we should be willing to serve, because God has called us to do so.

It is important that we take pride in our work. We are not supposed to seek recognition from those we serve, although a pat on the back once in a while helps, but we are to know that the one who called us will exalt us in due time. The simple life calls us to serve willingly. Clergy will do well to establish themselves as servants rather than bosses, executives, or the one always in charge. My desire is to be your servant in giving you what I believe is beneficial for you. After I became semi-retired, my wife and I found a church we wanted to attend. After attending for a while, we decided this church would be home to us. I spoke to both the pastor and his associate, explaining that I only sought to be a servant. I wasn't seeking any recognition for my years in ministry, or for my titles. I say this to let you know how strongly I feel about being a servant for Christ. There is freedom in being a servant. The secular world will not understand this. Sometimes, Christians don't understand it. I have had challenges getting Bible study groups to understand this concept. It is biblical. It is not something that I came up with on my own. For some persons, it means giving up their independence or autonomy. Most likely, we don't understand it as new converts. We grow or mature into the understanding.

We live in a *do nothing for nothing* society. Everyone expects to get paid for what they do for someone else. We seem to have gone far from the time when neighbors helped neighbors without having to be asked. Folks cared deeply for one another. If a house or barn burned, neighbors helped rebuild. If someone lost their job, friends made sure the family had food. Friends and neighbors became servants to those in need.

Some persons were known to take time off work to help a sick friend. What has happened to us? Where is our compassion? Where is the love of God that is supposed to be in our hearts? Clergy can ask themselves the same questions. Once again, I am not trying to be judgmental but just state facts. I know not all clergy want to be a servant. Some of us resist anyone telling us what to do. Maybe we have not considered the freedom that comes with being a servant of Christ. Maybe we are still too independent. When will we let go and let God have control of the reins?

For clergy to be servants means we do not seek positions of authority and power. We do not wish to lord it over others. We simply want to serve. Can it be simpler than that? It means we look beyond the faults of others and see their needs. We will quickly forgive those who wrong us. We will work to restore a fallen brother or sister to the faith. We will remember that to be a servant means we will seek to make life better for others. Each day, we will ask ourselves what we can do to make life better for someone that day. In II Corinthians 12:15 (KJV), Paul says, "And I will gladly spend and be spent for you; though the more abundantly I love you, the less I be loved." We need to be like Paul, loving unconditionally and not expecting anything in return. There are times when we don't get a "Thank you." That must not deter us; we must look at it as human error. We will see a lot of them. How simple is it to want to be a servant instead of a leader? Don't misunderstand me. I know as clergy we are leaders, but how do we come across to those we lead? Our actions need to show we wish the best for everyone.

Clergy might get the impression they might be taken advantage of if they are too open to the giving of themselves. None of us want to be put upon in excessive ways. However, we need to understand that our role is to give ourselves to others and to help in spiritual ways in which we can. We must realize that even if we are taken advantage of, it doesn't take anything away from our character, of who we are, if we can only see God has made us rich in him so that we can distribute to others. There might be times when we feel we have little to give. At those times, let us be reminded of Jesus and his disciples. On several occasions, Jesus would take a small portion of food, give it to his disciples, and tell them to feed the crowds of people. A miracle would happen. All the people would be fed, with portions left over. Can we, clergy, expect the same? I believe we should. God is still the same God, although earthly situations have changed somewhat. He can still take the little that we have and make it something fit for supplying persons' needs.

Early in my ministry, actually in my first pastorate, I was challenged to trust God with the use of little. I was a bivocational pastor. My weekly pay from the church was fifty-two dollars. On one particular Sunday night, I was given my pay before leaving the church: As my wife and I started down the highway to our house, I heard a voice tell me Sister Grace needed that money. I told my wife, and she exclaimed, "All of it?" I said, "Yes, all of it." I later made a trip to Grace's house and told her what the Lord had spoken to me. She was thankful, because that was the exact amount of money she needed to pay two bills. I was amazed at how God had worked. I still stand amazed at his power to solve problems for us, but I have learned to trust him more. By the way, my wife and I never missed the money. God also supplied our financial needs. I don't tell you this story to brag about any of my feats in faith but to show how God can work through us—if we are willing to be the servants he desires us to be. All of us can recall times when we saw the miraculous happen. We should never forget what God does for us and through us. Many are waiting to hear our encouraging stories. We can be the hope-givers to a discouraged world.

Often, I think about what legacy I will leave behind when I pass from this world. I question myself about it. None of us want to pass from the scene of life and leave nothing behind for others, especially for our family. We concern ourselves with life insurance policies large enough to take care of our family at our demise. We get our wills in order. We try to save money and invest wisely to take care of ourselves and our families. We feel good about it all. Then we ask ourselves if that is enough. We often feel like something is missing. In fact, something *is* often missing. The missing ingredient is that we haven't provided for a personal legacy about our faith in God, or how we are to live as a servant to God. If I can leave anything behind that will be most valuable for my daughter, I wish to leave her with my faith in God's miraculous power. From my personal spiritual journal, I hope to show those left behind how I trusted the Lord with my life and how God came through for me on many occasions. Most of all, I want to teach them to be a servant. Sure, someone will get all the books in my library and all my musical instruments in my music room, with all my music CDs. Even the degrees that hang on the wall will be left for someone to look at or store away somewhere. But what of my personal self will be left in the memories that will speak the loudest about me? I pray it will be those memories about my servanthood. What is your wish for your family's memories?

I have fond memories of my childhood, when the family was gathered around the table in the dining room for the Sunday meal. Quite often, there were guests present. My mother or one of my sisters would be dashing around, serving up food to the guests. It seemed to be their duty to make sure everyone at the table got plenty to eat. Whether they realized it or not, they were our *servants*. They received joy in doing that work. When everyone got up from the table, exclaiming how full they were and how good the meal was, my mother was fully paid. Is it that way with clergy? Are we content to dish out the needed spiritual food for the hungry? There are plenty of hungry people out there. In fact, many are starving spiritually. There is no need for it with all the spiritual food we have available. But how well are we serving it? Do we make folks feel welcome at the table? I am not referring specifically to the Sunday sermon, although it could fit here, but to our total calling to be a servant.

Epilogue

To be called to teach and preach God's Word and to nurture and give pastoral care to God's children is a high calling. I know of no higher calling. We are called to help those who are struggling. In this business (God's business), we should be accustomed to giving help to others. That is our calling. That is our purpose. That is who we are: servants of God. And it is vitally important we have a clear vision of what the journey will require.

It does make a huge difference how we meet the hurting world. Can people see our sincerity and love? Is there grace in our every action? Do we have abundant joy in our work? Have we let the daily stresses of the job rob us of our joy? How do we view our work and the pursuit of wealth? Do we expect to get rich monetarily, or are we seeking riches in heaven? Where is our heart in all this? Remember, it is necessary that we listen for the voice of God daily.

Living the simple life doesn't always seem so simple, does it? My intention has been to keep it *all* simple. I don't want to make any of it complicated for you. I feel strongly about clergy's intentional desire to be Christian on purpose. I believe our lives deserve examination under the light of the Holy Spirit in order for us to know how we are doing for God.

Do we remember when we first received our call to the ministry?

We probably remember our joy. Maybe we had anxiety and fear about it. Perhaps we had excitement over our first appointment as pastor to a church or to some other ministry. Through the years, many of us have suffered various difficulties and hardships in the ministry. How is our vision now? Are we still excited over new ministries to which God calls us? Have the burdens grown so heavy that we want to quit? We have the responsibility of being committed to God's calling. Whatever hinders us from giving our best to our ministry needs to be removed. There is someone out there who is waiting for an exciting, knowledgeable, inspired, and caring leader to provide guidance in understanding how to serve God. Let us cast off all that hinders us, and let us run swiftly to that person with the Good News of Jesus Christ. I pray that all of us experience a renewal in Christ. May we renew our vows to him and capture a new vision of the simple life.

About the Author

M. C. Tolbert has been a pastor, a teacher, an evangelist, and an adjunct professor of the Old Testament for Life Christian University. He holds a master's of divinity degree from Emory University and a doctorate of theology from Southwest Bible College and Seminary. He and his wife reside on Lookout Mountain in Georgia.

ENDNOTES

1. Richard J. Foster, *Celebration of Discipline*. New York: Harper San Francisco, 1998, 79–80.

2. Louis O. Caldwell, *Good Morning Lord: Meditations for Modern Marrieds*. Grand Rapids, Mich.: Baker House, 1974, p. 3.

3. Oswald Chambers, *My Utmost for His Highest: Prayer Edition*. Grand Rapids, Mich.: Discovery House, 1994, p. 65.

4. Caldwell, p. 4.

5. Albert C. Outler & Richard P. Heitzenrater, eds., *John Wesley's Sermons*. Nashville: Abingdon Press, 1991, 458–459.

6. Foster, p. 80.

7. Ibid, p. 4.

8. Howard Rice, *The Pastor as Spiritual Guide*. Nashville: Upper Room Books, 1998, 192.

9. Nell W. Mohney, *Don't Put a Period Where God Put a Comma*. Nashville: Dimensions for Living, 1993, 38–41.

10. The Optimist Creed is from Optimist International and taken from a brochure of the Optimist Club of Greeneville, Tennessee.

11. Reggie McNeal, *A Work of Heart*. San Francisco: Jossey-Bass Publishers, 2000. 187.

12. Leonardo Boff, *When Theology Listens to the Poor*. San Francisco: Harper & Row, 1998, 132–133.

13. Rodney J. Hunter, general ed., *Dictionary of Pastoral Care and Counseling*. Nashville: Abingdon Press, 1990, 956.

CPSIA information can be obtained at www.ICGtesting.com
Printed in the USA
LVOW13s1820081113

360517LV00002B/172/P